Laney Leighanne

A Father's Daughter

I thank My mom for being my lifeline during the hardest time of my life, you were my rock even when you were cracking. I thank Mrs. Connor for hearing me when I felt invisible. I thank my friends, high school and college. Lastly, I dedicate this book to my late father, my feelings are as shown. "Nothing stinks like a pile of unpublished writing." Sylvia Plath.

Table Of Contents

Needle

Needle in a haystack
so unreachable
yet so tempting
many ignore it
but you.

you found it
you used it
and you became
that needle.

we all looked for you
dug through the haystack
but you
you didn't want to be found.

you loved being lost
so much that
once we found you
you were already

rusted
broken
and even worse
Dead.

- your only daughter

After-Thought

I lay here in this
cold room, this
stiff bed, and under these
thin blankets.
Waiting for you.

the clock reads 11:30.

I can't see
I can't move
I can hear.
I can almost hear you.

are you there?
are you crying?
why are you crying, dear?
"Why, Dad?"

"oh, that's right.."
I realize my mistake.
too late?
Maybe.

my hands,
cold
my body,
stiff
my blood,
Thin.

time of death, 10:39
-your daughter, an hour too late.

Blue Truth

I hate hermit crabs.
Their shell, shielding them from the world.
The hard covering, casually painted over.
The reds, blues, pinks, and purples
covering the natural ugly.

The pinks may shield the brighter shells
as the blues cover the darker.
if you were a hermit crab
your shell would be painted blue.

A man of his shell.
The blue, covering the colors
with an ominous aura.
No one wants to see the true darkness
of you.

You had your shell to hide.
to hide when you told me to never do drugs.
to hide when you told me not to go to
parties.
to hide when you wanted more than just
a cigarette.

"Why would someone hide after telling you
these things?"

because
The shell was there to shield their own truth.
Not only was the shell ugly, but it was
covered.
covered in a new hard covering

painted blue, shielding the ugly brown.

then there's you, hiding in your
ugly, brown, and painted shell.

your
shield
from your own true self.

I hate hermit crabs.
Their shell shielded them from the world.
The hard covering, casually painted over.
The reds, blues, pinks, and purples
covered the natural ugly.
The pinks shielded the brighter shells
as the blues covered the darker.

Prescence

Today is an off day.
I follow you as usual
I talk to you as usual
but you never notice.

Clean your room.
Do the dishes.
Take out the trash.
Why are you procrastinating?

You lay there not even looking at me
Have I failed you again?
I know I wasn't great a year ago
but I'm better now.
I'm clean, I'm here
why do you disregard me
dear?

Clean your room.
Do the dishes.
Take out the trash.
Why are you not listening!

I heard you say
"I miss my dad a little more today"
But I'm here?
I have been here!
I have been screaming for you
to listen.

But you disobey
This has always been a thing

every single day.
Today is not an off day
you choose to cause this
dismay

You always went against me
but I understood then.
I was no father, nor parent.
I was not there, but I'm here
now.

Right?

Right? I'm here!
I talk to you every day
I follow you every which way
so why miss me?

The day continues
You go home, and you lay there..
You have homework but you change into
warmer clothes
why? the house is warm.
You have no plans but put on shoes
Why?

You get in the car, solemnly.
Where do you plan to go?
you turn on the music you hated
but I love.
10 minutes down the road we pull in.

Today is an off day.
You sit down in the way you do
legs crossed, back sulked.

next to the grave in front of you
why are we at a cemetery on
October 6, 2022?

Here lies a beloved father-
You cry silently, I rub your back
your tears never ceased to stop.
you never ignored me
you were alone, in your-
world.
As I am on another plane-
I'm still stuck on my own
death date.

I will continue following you
To be the father I wish I was
It's been fun, being stuck in
October 2021.

- love, dad.

Goodnight

It's cold out here
I wonder how you are.
I lay here staring at the stars
deep into the dark night.

The stars are different than the ones you see
but maybe you look at them and think of
me?
You don't see them often, maybe small
instances
when they're below your feet, I know you're
around often
but I still can't see.

Why is it always night, not for you, but me?
You talk about the flowers that supposedly
surround me?
Almost as far as the eye can see
but I feel like you're lying, is this what death
has come to be?

I stare at the dark gray stars every night,
only I can see
wondering why you only talk to me at night
isn't it late? It's way past your bedtime.
Talk to me during the day; this is where
your father draws the line.

What dad would I be? letting you out so late
are you not afraid?
of what turn each night will take?

People are dangerous, you should be at
home
Safe.

Instead, you talk to me, regularly, every
single day.
Maybe it isn't night, maybe I just ran out of
time
maybe I'm just staring at these
concrete lines, lining where I lay today
and tomorrow
and the next day.

But in my mind, you're coming out to see
me at night.
You seem angry when I don't respond,
but darling it's dark outside, and I don't want
to be the one
to wake up the birds, covering the trees.

I'll talk to you in the morning sweetie
please go to sleep.
pull the covers tight, and tell Mom
goodnight
I'll talk to you in the morning
and in the daylight.

-Love you, Dad.

Hero

I know you resent me
I know you wish you could hit me
I know you wish you could scream
I know you wish I wasn't so mean.

I love how you look just like me
my beautiful daughter, wind blows your hair
like a sail over the sea.
I see everything in you, from me.

I wish you could see how my eyes gleam
every time I hear your laugh-filled screams
I wish you could see how fast I ran
when you fell into the
3-feet-deep sea.

Though no challenge for me, I'd be your
hero
the man to save you from the
oh, so scary ocean.
A blanket of blue.
I love you.

Now you can swim with more motion
you shave your legs, and you can cook.
You've become my beautiful potion.
my prize in which could deceive the skies
to be the sun in its cloud-filled eyes.

So pretty, so sweet, your eyes gleam with
the light

rays of sun put up no fight, to how bright
you've always shined.
My beautiful daughter, how I wish you
could've understood my mind.

I'll still be there to save you
from that blanket of blue.
this time it's tears
from a boy who could never understand you.

I have my tissue
and I have my boots
I'll make sure this blanket of blue
will never consume you.

for I am your hero
I'll never let you down
and I will continue to show
that I am a dad, and I love you so.

My beautiful daughter
never let this blanket of blue
consume you.
I'm no longer able to save you; I can only
watch
my fight is over, and it was my actions to
botch.

my beautiful daughter, you make me proud
it's all on you now
show me what being a hero is all about.
for which I'll always love you in the turn-
around.

- your hero,

My Dear Door

I don't want to fix you anymore
for which you are a closed door.
Never to be opened, but adored.
You're still broken, used again and again.
a token, for an arcade, you were a door I'd
go through
every single day.

I saw you often, through the hottest of days
You and I would play
open, close, open, close
those were the days my mind could doze
no stress, no worries, wind in my hair, snot
in my nose.

One day, I never used that door again.
Whether it was my age or the acne on my
face
me and the door grew astray.
You were always ajar, and I was never too
far away
For which I still saw you, every single day.
sometimes, I wish life didn't make us depart
this way.

Time went on, and you rusted.
became a door I no longer trusted
the knob, old and moldy
the hinges screaming, "Fold me! Fold me!"
The realization hit me: I hadn't seen you.
I saw you, but I didn't see, you.

The door being long in the tooth
I tried to get it to move
in which there was one such movement
then, in that moment, I found amusement.
I could only close the door, now it was
barred.

This door to never be opened was heart-
rending
for which I never saw this ending
I could never fix you; too intricate, too old
to fix you would be too bold.

I couldn't risk cracking you.
This failure enveloped me.
I missed this door, for which it held my dear
childhood
I couldn't understand why I must go through
such, tragedy.
I loved all you held and your beautiful, dark
wood.

This door was something that could never
leave
this wood so rare, this wood not to be found,
never should.
over time, I relished in the door's ability to
comfort
for which it's old wood would smile
only when I don't see, and once in a while.

my dear door saw me and my inner child

my dear door raised me, having watched me
be so
young and wild.
I don't want to fix you anymore
for which you are a closed door.
Never to be opened, but adored.

Little Girl

I'll be better soon, I promise, little girl.
For you, my entire world, I'd sink all the
ships, watch them swirl.
No, I haven't stopped yet, but here's a new
pet!
For I'll be clean, before I pat him on the
head
He'll lick my hand with a look saying,
"You're a good man."

I'll be better soon, I promise, little girl.
and when I am, the sun will shine, onto your
brown curls.
I'll brush your hair, braid it with lace
then a kiss on your face will show you, I'm
in the right place.

My little girl, I promise I'll show you the
world.
I'll be better soon, I promise, little girl.
My eyes have sunk, and I know things are
glum.
My watch is getting loose, but I'll always
have time for you
I'll buy you new shoes, lace them up, and
watch you run
We can even fish; that's my final wish: you,
me, and the sun.

I'll be better soon, I promise, little girl.
I can the see clouds, the sun, and birds so
clear

I'll take a picture and send it to you dear
just let me find my phone
I always have it; where did I leave it alone?

My little girl, in this picture I send
you'll see the clouds that never end.
The birds flying in the wind
and me, your father, and your best friend.

My Daylily

my Daylily is dead.
no longer yellow like the sun
only yellow like a day drinker, after a short
run.
the bugs have won, destroying you more and
more than day one.

my Daylily is dead.
wilted and fallen onto the dark
decomposition-filled dirt.
my flower. once so inadequately pretty, now
an ugly yellow.
once filling me with contentment
now filling me with disgust.

my "You're So Silly" is dead.
once loud and carrying it's leaves with
confidence.
its petals were soft to touch, bringing
comfort to those around
however, you became weak, the sun became
strong and your bugs
tore you apart.

my Dad-ily is dead.
my flower used to flutter in the wind,
compete to win, and held me so tight I felt
like an Oreo thin.
once yellow like the bright sun, now yellow
like a rotten lemon
smelly and glum.

my Dad is dead.
disgustingly gone.
an ugly yellow, leaving a bad taste to those
he was fond.
I miss my flower; I could plant a garden full
of Daylilies.

not a single one would be My Daylily
not a single one would be my "you're so
silly"
not a single one would be my Dad-ily.
not a single one would be my Dad.
for his wilting will always kill me
and another flower will never fulfill me.
I loved my Daylily.

Green

You were so easily wisped away
a light blow onto you, and there you'd sway
with the wind, into the skies, out of the view
of my brown eyes.

Light will never shine the way it did when
you were in my line of sight.
I wish the water didn't sound so calm
I wish the air didn't feel so warm
I wish the sky wasn't so blue
for I have nothing left of you.

So why should the sky be so bright
why should the grass be so green
and why should the entire world be so pretty
and sweet
when you're not with me.

The world was so mean when you were
here.
You noticed the cracks in the concrete
while I took refuge from the grass beneath
my bare feet.
You wallowed in the dirty looks of passer-
bys
while I smile at those whose eyes never met
mine.

I loved the world; the world loved me.
You loved the world, but like a dandelion
it'd blow its wind
and knock you off your unbalanced feet.

Dirt in a windstorm
you blew away, never to be seen.

Pollen in the early spring
you clung to my toes only to be wiped away
by the soft green
beneath my feet.

Now I see the hollow holes
covering the bark of a tree.
For it calls to me to find something to fill
this wound
but every rock, every pebble, and every root
I'd give
nothing would ever be the same as the shiv
that made it.

Why is the world so pretty when you're not
with me?
My skin burns from the salt, made by me
my eyes red from the stress, made by she
my hands sweat from the anxiety made by
the blue cloud
covering my head
the rain falls from it only hitting my cheeks.

it falls for so much time; I'm no longer
counting the weeks.
You've made me so weak.
I only see the ants crawling through the
concrete
stepping on everyone and twisting my toes

no longer green grass below my feet

only the dark grey, black soles, then my bare
feet
for the happiness from the soft green
will never be the same or mean
as much as it was when you were with me.

Alive

A dark, gray box.
Hollowed, dark, and almost empty
filled with the stories of you and memories
that will never be told.
For you grew too old, and your time couldn't
have ended more bold
now all that's left is what remains of you, in
this dead empty hole.

There's dandelions blowing all around you
green grass flourishing just inches away
from where you lay.
Ant beds nearby all full of life and just
trying to survive.

I hate these living things, for my dad is
surrounded by everything

Alive.

Memory Lane

I walk down the same path every single
night.
Once I shut my eyes, the path begins, and
my heart sinks.
The same dark walls filled with words
each detrimental
some even mental
then a few sentimental.

There's pictures plastered all over
even strands of clothes I presumed my
"lucky clover."
Each time there's two different paths to
choose, I go left
for every left turn starts with moments of me
I want to see

clearly.

When I go right
My heart turns, and my eyes burn to the
sights
for I see the things that have scarred me so
deeply.
The trauma I push back.. all of the above
but these are still moments I love.

Left or right, I still see a small yellow light
at the end of my path, there's a light I can't
ever seem to find
It's warm and enlightening

even when the things surrounding me are
frightening
this light motivates me to keep walking and
continue fighting.

I wish I could reach this light
every time I come close, I see photos of you
I can smile softly, knowing you're here now
but it's at that moment my eyes shoot open.

The remnants of my mind keep me busy
from time to time.
Only to hurt me when the daylight lights.
I wish for a few more moments
that I can reminisce
in the comfort of my head
even if my eyes burn a little red.

Regretful

An alarm rings in my head
screaming at me every night as I go to bed
my eyes sweat, and my cheeks burn red.
I wish I could change the last things I said.

I've wept and wept
over my embarrassing regret
but I can never seem to get my last text
out of my head

It flies through my mind
like a fly on a hot Friday night.
You taught me to never say bye without
looking them in the eye
and saying I love you
just in case they die.

However, all I could mutter
was something so hateful my mouth
deserved a disgusting gutter
where all my words would float to another
space
and I could even move on from your dead
face.

I beg and cry to the sky
to let me in with my disguise.
Just to the heavenly gates
holding your favorite food, used as my bait.
I wish I wasn't so late
your timely death might've just been fate.

I saw your bracelet, exhibiting your faith
how much happier could I be knowing
there's someone in the sky watching you
breathe
but that person will never be me.

I hate the sky that's blue as much as I hate
the sea
for you are not with me when I look at either
of thee.
My last words to you
so full of hate
there's nothing in this world that could
replace
how much I hate myself for treating you in
such a bad way.
I miss you so much
I think of you at every lunch
I see you as my crutch
for I'm burdened by my choices
that I've always regretted so much.

Thought Bubble

I have a constant thought bubble over me.
filled with flashbacks of you and I
The red dirt getting in my eyes
me and you getting "lost" in the backyard,
looking up at the blue sky.

I wish it would go away.
I despise being stuck in my head, day by day
I always tend to miss the way the trees sway
in the wind, they rustle, reminding me of
you and my mother's struggle

to get along, listening was like hearing an
out-of-tune song.
But I always heard
nosey like a little bird
I'd listen and cry the majority of those loud,
never-ending nights.

Maybe if I wasn't so stuck in my mind
I would've learned how to rewind time
to stop you from falling from that tree at 8 or
9
that morning. We were going to church
you were frustrated with some birds
climbed your ladder, then got hurt.

I was scared, but you still patted me on my
shirt.
Maybe if this bubble would pop
I could make time stop
in a time when you were still alive

give you a hug, then say my goodbyes.

That would make my life so much less filled
with lies.
Or maybe more, I mean my last words to
you weren't too adored.
I was angry, but that's no excuse.
I wish I could change the things I said to
you.

Maybe you would know, or already do
I love you, and I miss you.
I wish there was more I could do.

I wish the ladder was how you died.

Not the needle; I wish the drugs weren't
your demise.
But like the birds that made you yell angry
cries
the memories of that moment would be
brighter in my eyes.

You'd know I loved you so very much
You'd know I had no regrets of my words
over a previous lunch
and we'd have fresh, happy memories.

Now? not so much.

Unanswered Wishes.

A sunny afternoon, bright and no trace of
gloom.
Sunday morning, loud music between 6 am
to 2.
Tuesday night, reminiscing on the daylight.
Friday evening, lightly sleeping.

Memories of you, from colored
to a shade of blue.
Slowly I forget, every minute we spent
singing your songs, you correcting where I
was wrong.

I remember all parts of you
good or bad, each weighing on my back
I wish for one minute to relapse.
Where your hand and mine could clasp
for one second.
Is that too much to ask?

When you laid in your death bed, I held your
hand.
Though at that moment, you were just a
man.
Not my dad, not my best friend
just a shell, maybe even an empty can.

Filled with memories, never to be told
all just because you got old.
I still ask for signs, never to be answered.
It's been over a year now, and I'm stuck in
my mind

Swallowed by the memories, I can call mine
but drowned out by the sighs, I make every
time.

I can't hear your voice anymore.
I can barely remember your face.
the memories are there, slowly being erased.
Grieving is so hard; I feel so alone
and all I can think about is your rotting
bones.
So far, yet so close

the only thing between us is words someone
wrote.
On a wall in front of me, because your
family didn't get you a plot
though they have the money, just not the
thought.
I hope your ashes never blow away
I couldn't imagine watching you leave me
again one day.

You weren't the best, even when they laid
you to rest
but I always relished the idea
you were bad
a little less.

maybe soon, we can hug again
and me and you can be best friends
You can tell me stories that never end
even walk me down an isle, to someone you
trust
with your daughter to someone she loves

There's so many wishes that will never come true
one being me, talking to you.
The sad part about wishes, they never come true
it's just a reminder I'll never see you.

I'll never stop loving you for who you were
not for who you became
for I never knew you that way
"He's a bad man," Old you, would say
what a hypocrite.

I shouldn't think this way.
I know your faults.
But I love them most.
For my dad taught me lessons that I shouldn't boast.
I love you to the moon dad, I love you the most.
Though you weren't the best, I'd hope to see your ghost.

I was your little girl; I still am today.
I wish for my feelings to go away.
I wish for my memories to forever stay.
and I wish for my dad to come back one day.

from, bug

Tree Bark

A tree with no bark.
The inner layer left unprotected
each bug leaving its mark
the tree never made it.

A girl with no father
her standards never high
she'd fall in love with the sky
if it could say, "I love your eyes."

Her mind fogged by romantic movies and
books.
"This is love," as she looks to the corny
tropes
those of which hold her heart by a rope.
She'd fall in love, be used, and begin to
mope.

Filling a hole, never having a bottom.
If the ocean said, "I love your hair,"
She'd pour water into the ocean until it
overflowed.
She'd fill our atmosphere, empty of any
more air.

She yearns for love in every wrong corner
Each year, they'd almost call a coroner
hopeless romance, for her, a dangerous
dance
She'd forgive and forget, each man's words
having her in a trance.

Her mother would beg
for her to have a level head
"Don't love them because of what they said"
She begs for her to love them behind their
actions
not because her cheeks burned a little red.

She'd have moments of peace
where she sits outside with the leaves
of the bark-less trees, admiring their strength
to never go away; however, she didn't know
on the inside of each was only decay.

Her optimistic mind kept her afloat
the sea beneath her, lightly brushing her
toes.
There's a shark nearby, ready to rock her
boat
she thinks it's a fish, she can only see his
nose.

Blue Can

You held a blue can
night after night; it'd have a small gleam.
It's the light from the moon and the stars
overhead you, just a man.
You and your Bud Light can, sitting
solemnly on the patio, you not so keen.

I remember the smell of your breath after
you'd drank with your friends.
I remember the yell of your voice when
Mom would ask questions.
I remember the sound of the bells that went
off when you slammed the doors.
My mom loved those bells, the rings would
be silenced from the yells.

The house would shake, my mother's dinner
in the oven, continuing to bake.
The house would shake, my small heart
would continue to break.
The house would shake, my dogs would
whine and cry like a stray.
The house would shake, my hands clasped
together as I'd pray.

The night would pass, and the sun would
rise
I'd walk outside to see what caused such a
big fight
your blue can lay in the dew of the morning
gloom

filled with your sorrows, you may drink
more tomorrow.

I associate the smell of beer with you.
I go to parties and think of you, the smell
and the gloom.
Others holding the blue can to my face, it's
almost like you want me to take your place.
I always denied, for my little prayers still
ring in my mind.

The metal of the can reminds me of a wall.
It's thin, but it won't fall
thin enough to hear through, thick enough
that no beer
seeps through.
I watch others down your favorite drink
each drop falling into their body; I can hear
their liver weep.

However, maybe their liver's cries
are drowning out the tears coming from their
eyes?
It's a party, it's hot. I shouldn't assume things
are something they're not.
Who would cry while drinking a beverage
that's there to numb the pain inside?

The pain inside.

Each drop a small bandage for the things
deep within
like a metal can; its walls are thin.

thin enough to hear through, thick enough
that no beer
seeps through.
Could this be true?
Here I am, relating things to you.

I see you in others, but different fonts.
I see you in others, as they take shots.
I see you in others, as they drink in parking
lots.
I see you in others, after their parents have
fought.
I see you in others, as they tell me their
depressive thoughts.
I see you in others, different fonts.

You surround me, but you are gone
You are there, but I only see cons.
I never see a pro, a pro being you
I only see a con, a con being those who did
what you would do.

I watch each con drown their despair
I hear each con wish that someone was there
I smell each con as they walk past me; the
beer smell bare
I brush each con, damp with sweat, clothes
sticking to their arm hair
I can almost taste the stale beer in the air.

You're always there, reminding me of you
every time I see a small blue
can.

I can almost make out the saddest silhouette
of a
man.
There you are on the patio, drinking you-
know-what.
You held a blue can
inside; it was liquid
ready to fill the thin walls of such a sad
sorry man.

Unsaid

I am stuck in the words
I will never be able to say to you.
The silence between the wind
and the rustle of the trees; this is where I
cannot move.

I'm twirling in the breeze
just a dead leaf. spinning till I hit the ground
only being able to hope the wind takes me
again
and spins me round.

stuck between the gravity of my earth
and the force of the wind it's birthed
the planets watch from afar as I'm taken to
where I'd restart.

This will never be fair, for I can only grow
to die
never to be more than a leaf floating through
the sky.
stuck between the words I will never say to
you.
between the I and the L, I'm the space that's
sometimes there
for others tend to lead the "love you" all but
bare.

I acted like I never cared.
For you were never there.
You didn't deserve the love I gave, leaving
my own heart surrounded by empty air.

The cracks naturally made in a rock.
Those who collect, never to pick
for the rocks are pretty, but they've got a
nick.
The crack within holds the emptiness of its
end.

later to be turned to dust, the cracks leaving
it open to the world, unable to defend.
stuck between the words I cannot say.
If you were here, I'd still stray away.
For I know exactly why I felt such way.

Still, I wished for amends to be placed
I'll forever be stuck in the words that I could
never fully let out of my mouth.
For you never became a deserving man of
the daughter you didn't watch sprout.

Stairwell

I write and I write
each poem belonging to a fight
within myself
a piece of me
I've drug through hell.
I'm stuck in my head
yet this isn't a cry for help
maybe it is, but I'll always continue to write
through my yells.
Words engulf me, lost in the letters
A to Z each one surrounding me
and my mind, maybe this is my waste of
time
or it's my outlet, no electrical line.
They're listening, but are they really?
I'm screaming into an empty hole
constantly echoing throughout my soul
is anyone there, or am I in a room full of
blank stares?
My blindfold tight, held over my eyes
I can't see you but I see the light.
If there's light there's someone, so maybe
they're there.
I'll keep talking
and maybe I'll hear someone, walking?
I'm asking questions, I'm answering myself
I'm writing to you, but are you also in my
hell?
My mind ponders the things I cannot tell
for they scar me so deep, if you took a step
into me, you'd fall through a never-ending
stairwell.

Each bump you'd hit on the way
leaving bruises and cuts
none are ever enough
to break your fall
for this fall would fill your day.
Ever so deep, you'd see signs you can't read.
Then your eyes adjust
seeing through the dust
it's the mind of me, my memories consume
you
and now all you can do
is wallow within me.
Maybe if someone fell
I wouldn't be alone in this hell
please walk down my stairwell.
Talk to me, answer my questions.
I'm talking, can you hear me?
Can you read between the lines?
Or am I just another set of lines
that you only read on your free time?
God I hate it. I hate it all.
Please can someone fall?

Message to reader: I wrote the poem *Stairwell* in the darkest part of the grief. If you ever have suicidal thoughts or have thoughts about hurting yourself, it's okay to talk to someone. People care. People love you. Your life is worth living.

1-800-273-8255

Maybe

I am my own person.
That is until I see your nose on my face.
Until I see the hands that took your life
away..
on me. For I am you-- another version.

In the mirror, I seek
Your eyes to see me
Yet what I find is the replicate
of the man that didn't get it.

He had his dad, yet he wasn't fond
just like me, though, that apple didn't fall
wrong.
not far from the tree, is my dad and me.
only one that can weep.

Sometimes, I wonder if he just didn't want to
be a dad.
not to me, but just in general. Is it really that
bad?
To teach your daughter how to change a
tire?
Or to watch her maybe sing in a middle-
school choir?

Is it that scary to maybe see her smile on a
dewy morning?
Is it really better to watch her in mourning?
There are so many maybes in what could've
been

a girl and her dad, giggles and warmth, days
on end

Calloused

I am calloused.
My unforgiving denial of life
The dislike of what's kept me alive
I am calloused, yet I keep holding my hand
up to survive.

I began pristine yet impure.
Dirty hands but soft
I gave up, asking God to take me-- he did
not
I hold my hand, begging for a cure.

My soft hand begged and pleaded to be
taken
Yet he hands me a task
"Do this, and you will last."
I did what was asked. Though I was shaken

I reach my hand once again
this time a slight scratch on my palm
I told him it was hard and he was no friend
He said nothing and handed me my next
"calm."

I did what he said
Though I never bowed my head
He didn't listen to what I said was my end
He won't take me away; he left me to fend

I think of raising my hand
for the third time, I'm angry with his ears
as he's angry with my land

I begged and pleaded with tears
while he lied, "I'm a friend."

My hand raises
this time it's grabbed
But I can't feel the traces
that his light has mapped

My hand is calloused
He hands me a task
I do so with ease
I couldn't even see how fast
I only fell to my knees.

This realization has brought me tears
His hand ignores mine and wipes my own
fears.
What was I doing begging him for fewer
years?
I raised my hand again; this time, I pleaded
for his ears.

My hand hardened, no feeling given
Yet when I hold another
My feelings are driven
I notice now his goals are one from the other
My hand, once soft and defeated
Given trials, I was hurt and depleted
I thought this was my misery
Not what would rebuild me

He cut my hands; my palms were bleeding
When healed, they had no more feeling
for I could grab a cactus if he really needed

My hands are calloused; the hard way, I
never cheated
I hold what he gives, no more difficulty
within
I trust that there's a lesson to learn, at the
end
He taught me how to grow and defend
even when I felt like I was always
weakened.

The Tree's Leaves

I am a tree in a field of nothing.
My bark is thick, water barely seeps through
my leaves are untearable, defending me
from
people like you.

You don't near me often
but when you do, you mindlessly grab a leaf
a part of me.
rip it from my branch and go to squeeze it in
your hand

as you do you feel the leaf cut you.
you never noticed the thick shards this leaf
grew.
In the beginning, you'd tear my leaves with
ease.
each one crumbling in your hands and
falling past your knees.

you'd keep walking away, mindless as parts
of me fly away.
you did this time and time again.
each time you'd notice a slight difference in
my strength

you'd go to crumble my leaves
only to be stopped by the toughness of each
however they weren't strong enough then,
they'd crumble again.

The last time you hurt me

you ripped a leaf, squeezed and stopped in
your tracks
you watched my crumbs fall to the grass
unlike other times, you didn't keep your
pace fast.
you stopped and turned to me

admiring this tree
I almost felt like you finally noticed my
pretty leaves.
the ones regrowing, and the ones full at the
top.
I watched your hand drop, right above your
hip
a small red drop would drip
from your middle finger tip.

This day you came, I was ready for your
pain
to feel a small part of me easily ripped away.
you raised your hand, never giving me a
glance.
You grabbed a leaf and pulled with one
hand.
my leaf didn't budge, two hands it became.

You pulled and grunted, until it was ripped
away.
My leaf in your hands, as you walked on
I watched you ball your fist and listened to
your hummed song.

You stopped once again, this time I could
feel some dismay

you were balling your fist as blood spilled
away.
You began yelling and crying, for someone
to help

you couldn't open your fist
you couldn't crumble my leaf.
there you stood, slowly falling to your knees
shakily you laid down, your hand and my
leaf on the ground.

your fist came un-balled, my leaf with no
cracks.
You stopped moving or making noise
almost as if you were scorned.
Then I noticed
my leaf grew poisonous thorns.

I am a tree in a field of nothing.
My bark is thick, water barely seeps through
my leaves are untearable, defending me
from
people like you.

Dandelion

a little girl stumbles onto a dandelion
she picks it and thinks
her eyes glance to her dad as he winks
she takes a deep breath and blows, her laugh
a shriek.

three years go by
she's sees the soft white
she picks this dandelion and looks to her
side
her dad's soft smile, his beard now light.

six years passed
now she stands on the other side of glass
looking out, a coffin surrounded by grass
glancing down there's a dandelion growing
fast.

three-year anniversary
she's in a graveyard cursing
she yells and screams, a soft white ball is
lurking
her head falls weary, a dandelion grows - its
roots working.

a decade has flown
her heart now resewn
she stands with her head high and a white
rose
a tear falls from her nose right onto where a
new dandelion grows.

her little girl stumbles onto a dandelion
she picks it and thinks
her eyes glance to her mom, she's at the
brink
she takes a deep breath and blows
"I hope my mommy's heart is never weak."

Gone Skies

The skies are prettier now that you're gone.
an odd thought to have, yet it's fond.
I notice the blues when they disappear
I admire the pinks from this mountain up
here.

I stand on this cliff, noticing all that I
ignored
when I watched you slam the front door.
I see the green grass, I even thumb through
it
I pick the pretty shards sometimes,
wondering if I shouldn't.

Tears slowly fall from my eyes to the grass
the salt drying out the newly grown weeds
here I grieve your death, admitting it's true
at last
but denial felt better, I didn't need keep
wondering If you thought of me as you
passed.

I'm still on this cliff, looking at the sky
the colors have left me, darkness meets my
eye.
I look at the stars and wonder which you'd
pointed out
I'll never remember, I wish you'd told me
more than just north and south.

The sky's much prettier now that you're
dead.

A dark thought that constantly runs through
my head.
I wonder if this was your goal, to make me
see what's real.
but all you ever caused was the thought,
"No, Dad, you're not the man in this
hospital bed."

I hope you're okay
I leave the mountain after I pray
that maybe one day
my dad would be back to stay.

The Garden Within Her

My world didn't end when the lights were
dim.
My life wasn't over when my dad's fell to
the bin.
I was seventeen and felt my hope was thin.
I'm nineteen, and I can breathe again.

I never got over it
I learned to live
I never understood the joke; I thought it was
but I can sleep through the night with no
more fuss.

I miss my dad.
I miss my friend.
I miss the moments I thought would never
end
At seventeen, I was ready to see my dad
again.

I fell deeply into a pit of pain
I thought about every single way
I was ready to go
be called a no-show

Yet here I am, two years later my life with
no end.
I've cried, and I've thought about it again
I thought over it at eighteen; I didn't want to
fend.
I think when we don't know, our hearts do

I believe the heart will show you when it
wants to.

I was empty and hollow.
I never wanted to laugh.
I never wanted anything but to be first to go,
not last.
Yet when I tried, my heart said no.
I'm nineteen now, and I still miss my dad
Two years later, I still hear his laugh
It's okay to think of the past
But not relive it; that's when things are bad.

My world didn't end.
I stayed alive to fend.
I understood my heart when it told me to
stay and live.
I took my breath, and I let my deepest sighs
win.

I had a garden to water within me.
Every flower depended on the
girl with a hard patch; the girl is me.
I watered my garden, and each flower
bloomed.
The girl within me, finally, was no longer
consumed.

Daughterly

In another universe
I'm not my father's daughter.
I'm his childhood friend, he reminisces on as
a first
His first friendship never faltered.

We'd play in the trees
I'd trip and scrape my knees
He'd help me up, only for him to fall into the
leaves
we'd giggle and laugh like the kids we'd be

I'd have a better memory of him and me.
Maybe whoever my parents would be
would teach me lessons I could tell him
lessons that would've shaped him to be a dad
to me.

We'd play in the rivers, water splashing in
our eyes
he'd wipe his; I'd wipe mine
bugs would bite, and I'd probably cry
maybe he'd of known
how to comfort his daughter at night

Maybe he'd get mad that I rode his bike
Maybe he'd yell and scream through the
daylight
I'd calm him down and show him how not to
hit others
then maybe he'd know how to control his
anger toward his daughter's mother.

When someone told him to try the cigarette
on the ground
I could be there to say they're addictive and
shouldn't be around
He would've never become an addict
He would've been a father to his daughter;
no lies to hide that'd make him sick

In another universe, I wouldn't have been so
sad
I would've had an amazing dad
I would've never learned the lessons I have
I would've been so free, never trapped
to the idea of never having my best friend,
my dad.

In another universe, he'd be alive
He'd look at me and smile, telling me to
strive
My dad would be a man, not an addict trying
to be high
I would have my dad in another world
I'd have my heart together, never ripped
apart or hurled

In another universe, my dad and I would be
childhood friends
We'd grow up together and play till the
streetlight dims
I'd show him things he'd never been shown
I'd be his daughter and he never would've
known.

Message to the Reader.

For one, I'd like to thank you. Thank you for reading my book. All I want is for someone to read my words, to feel them.

I began writing this book in October 2021 after my father passed away. I was 17 years old and a junior in high school. His passing absolutely tore me to shreds. I was a completely different person after his death, and for a long time, it was in the worst way imaginable. I stopped sleeping, I stopped eating, I hung out with a bad crowd, and almost gave up my life-long dreams. My dad's death hung over my head like a noose.

When I began writing, I didn't know who I was writing to, or if anyone would ever read my poetry. I used it as my coping mechanism for a long time. I put the worst parts of my mind on paper and tore into myself in ways I don't even think I can explain. That time was truly the hardest time of my life.

When you read this book, I hope you feel a sense of feeling seen. If you have gone through something similar, I hope you feel heard. I know I'm just words on paper, but I hope you hear, see, understand, that I love you. You're unbelievably wanted in this world. Your worth in this world is unimaginable and no piece of paper, no small insult said from others, or no loss you might have should prove you different than what I'm saying now. You are here, you are breathing, and you are worth the breaths you are taking.

Life is full of a million turns, some with wrecks and some with the smoothest roads imaginable. You are driving and it's only the speed you go. Sometimes going too fast is scary and can hurt. It's okay to slow down and take a breath. It's okay to pull over and take a walk. It's okay to be you and be at your own pace.

If you ever have suicidal thoughts or thoughts of hurting yourself, please talk to someone. Once you're dead, you're dead forever. Take a breath and open your eyes to the world; it's so much prettier with your eyes open.

Thank you for reading. I love you.

Laney Leighanne.

Made in United States
North Haven, CT
21 May 2025

69074540R00060